Poppy

YOU HAVE A STORY TO SHARE

STORIES, MEMORIES AND MOMENTS
THAT HAVE SHAPED YOUR LIFE

The views and opinions expressed in this book are solely those of the author. Global Self Publishing is not to be held responsible for and expressly disclaims responsibility of the content herein.

Poppy, You Have a Story to Share
www.globalselfpublishing.com | Copyright © 2024
ISBN: 978-1-922664-76-1 (Paperback)   978-1-922664-77-8 (Hardback)

All rights reserved. Neither this book nor any parts within it may be sold or reproduced in any form or by any electronic or mechanical means, including information storage and retrieval systems, without permission in writing from the author. The only exception is by a reviewer, who may quote short excerpts in a review.

CONTENTS

POPPY, YOU HAVE A STORY TO SHARE

INTRODUCTION	POPPY'S INTRODUCTION
SECTION ONE	THE BEGINNING
SECTION TWO	GROWING UP
SECTION THREE	WHEN I WAS...
SECTION FOUR	PARENTHOOD
SECTION FIVE	LIFE, TRAVEL AND ADVENTURE
SECTION SIX	MEMORIES AND STORIES
SECTION SEVEN	MY FINAL WORDS

POPPY
YOU HAVE A STORY TO SHARE

INTRODUCTION

Every parent has a story to tell, although many are never provided with the opportunity to share or capture those special memories, moments and stories in one place.

This journal has been carefully designed so grandfathers can share their life stories and provide the answers to many questions that family and friends have never asked.

Poppy, use this journal to share your wonderful life. Your stories, memories, and moments will remain a keepsake for generations to come.

POPPY'S INTRODUCTION

A Message From Poppy

Poppy's Introduction

A message before I begin.

_____
_____
_____
_____
_____
_____
_____
_____
_____
_____
_____
_____
_____
_____

FULL NAME   DATE

Family Tree

Great-Grandmother   Great-Grandmother

Great-Grandfather   Great-Grandfather

Grandmother   Grandfather

Mother

Me

SECTION ONE
THE BEGINNING

POPPY - YOU HAVE A STORY TO SHARE

BABY YEARS

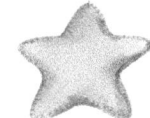

Full name at birth _____

Date of birth _____

Home address when born? _____
_____

Mothers name _____

Fathers name _____

The background to my birth name.
_____
_____
_____
_____

POPPY - YOU HAVE A STORY TO SHARE

My fathers age when I was born _____

Nationality _____

My fathers occupation _____

My mothers age when I was born _____

Nationality _____

My mothers occupation _____

Names and ages of my siblings (if applicable)
_____
_____
_____

Were you in good health as a baby?
_____
_____

Names of uncles and/or aunt's when you were born (as applicable)
_____
_____
_____
_____

POPPY - YOU HAVE A STORY TO SHARE

Share with us some information about your parents.

_____
_____
_____
_____
_____
_____
_____
_____
_____
_____

Grandparent Details

Mothers side.

Grandmother _____ Nationality _____

Grandfather _____ Nationality _____

Fathers side

Grandmother _____ Nationality _____

Grandfather _____ Nationality _____

POPPY - YOU HAVE A STORY TO SHARE

This is something that you may not know about our family history.

POPPY - YOU HAVE A STORY TO SHARE

Use these pages to include any photos or further information about your family or baby years.

POPPY - YOU HAVE A STORY TO SHARE

SECTION TWO
GROWING UP

POPPY - YOU HAVE A STORY TO SHARE

CHILDHOOD YEARS

What is your earliest memory as a child?

_____
_____
_____
_____
_____

Were you told of any funny things or unique characteristics you had as a toddler?

_____
_____
_____
_____
_____
_____

POPPY - YOU HAVE A STORY TO SHARE

As a toddler, what games or activities did you like to play?
_____
_____
_____
_____

What was your favourite toy growing up?
_____
_____
_____
_____

Did you have a pet or any pets as a young child?
_____
_____
_____
_____

POPPY - YOU HAVE A STORY TO SHARE

Did you have a favourite television show you loved to watch as a child?

_____
_____
_____
_____

What was your favourite book or books that you loved as child?

_____
_____
_____

Do you recall being involved in any accidents or hurting yourself as a young child? If so, is there a story behind the accident or injury?

_____
_____
_____
_____
_____
_____
_____

POPPY - YOU HAVE A STORY TO SHARE

Was there a moment you recall getting into big trouble as a child? Was there a punishment?

_____
_____
_____
_____
_____
_____
_____
_____
_____

Was there a special celebration that you recall attending as a child?

_____
_____
_____
_____
_____
_____

POPPY - YOU HAVE A STORY TO SHARE

What are your fondest memories between the ages of 5 - 12?

POPPY - YOU HAVE A STORY TO SHARE

Use these pages to include any childhood photos.

POPPY - YOU HAVE A STORY TO SHARE

Use these pages to include any childhood photos.

POPPY - YOU HAVE A STORY TO SHARE

What was your favourite meal as a child?

Did you have any close friends as a child? If so, please provide some names and details.

Was there a sport or special interest that you started participating in at a young age?

POPPY - YOU HAVE A STORY TO SHARE

EARLY SCHOOL YEARS

My elementary/primary school was called...

Provide the school location details.

Describe your school. Was it in a city or rural location? Was it large or small? What were some of the backgrounds of the children that attended?

POPPY - YOU HAVE A STORY TO SHARE

Was there a teacher that really stood out to you that made an impact on your childhood or education?

___

Provide details of your most memorable moment or story from your early school years.

___

POPPY - YOU HAVE A STORY TO SHARE

Did you have any close friends at school?

_____
_____
_____
_____
_____

What kind of student were you? Were you well-behaved or mischevous?

POPPY - YOU HAVE A STORY TO SHARE

What were your favourite subjects?

_____
_____
_____

Was there anything that you found challenging or difficult during your early school years?

_____
_____
_____
_____
_____
_____
_____
_____
_____
_____
_____

POPPY - YOU HAVE A STORY TO SHARE

Use these pages to include any photos or further notes from your early school years.

POPPY - YOU HAVE A STORY TO SHARE

Use these pages to include any photos or further notes from your early school years.

POPPY - YOU HAVE A STORY TO SHARE

TEENAGE YEARS

Describe what you were like as a teenager.

What were your key interests?

POPPY - YOU HAVE A STORY TO SHARE

Did you date anyone in your teenage years? If so, share some details or a story.

_____
_____
_____
_____
_____
_____
_____
_____
_____
_____

Is there anything you regret doing as a teenager?

_____
_____
_____
_____
_____
_____
_____
_____
_____
_____

POPPY - YOU HAVE A STORY TO SHARE

When and where did you learn to drive a vehicle?

At what age did you get your vehicle licence?

What was your first vehicle/mode of transport that you purchased?

Share an experience from your early years of driving.

POPPY - YOU HAVE A STORY TO SHARE

Use this page to include a photo of a vehicle you have owned.

POPPY - YOU HAVE A STORY TO SHARE

Was there a particular kind of music that you enjoyed listening to in your teens?

___

What was a favourite movie from your teens?

___

What were some of the hobbies or activities that you enjoyed most as a teenager?

___

POPPY - YOU HAVE A STORY TO SHARE

Was there a special holiday destination that you visited? If so, provide some details.

_____
_____
_____
_____
_____
_____
_____
_____
_____
_____
_____

List 3 words that best describe you as a teenager?

1.

2.

3.

POPPY - YOU HAVE A STORY TO SHARE

Did you attend High School? If so, where was it located and what was it called?

_____
_____
_____

What subjects did you enjoy at High School?

_____
_____
_____

Did you have a close friendship group? If so, provide some names and details.

_____
_____
_____
_____
_____
_____
_____
_____

POPPY - YOU HAVE A STORY TO SHARE

Describe one of your most memorable accomplishments at school.
_____
_____
_____

Did you have a nickname at school?
_____
_____

With what you know now, would you have done anything differently as a teenager?
_____
_____
_____
_____
_____
_____
_____

POPPY - YOU HAVE A STORY TO SHARE

Use this page to include any High School photos or extra details.

POPPY - YOU HAVE A STORY TO SHARE

Do you have any other stories, memories or moments from your teenage years that you would like to share?

_____
_____
_____
_____
_____
_____
_____
_____
_____
_____
_____
_____
_____
_____
_____

SECTION THREE
WHEN I WAS..

POPPY - YOU HAVE A STORY TO SHARE

When I was a child, I always looked forward to....

_____
_____
_____

When I was a teenager, I always dreamed of becoming...

_____
_____
_____

When I was a teenager, the biggest news story I can recall was...

_____
_____
_____

When I was growing up, my three favourite movies were...

1. _____
2. _____
3. _____

POPPY - YOU HAVE A STORY TO SHARE

When I completed school, the year was... _____

When I turned 21 yrs, I celebrated by....

_____
_____
_____

When I was in my teens, the silliest thing I did was.....

_____
_____
_____

When I was in my teens, I had a celebrity crush on....

_____
_____

When I was growing up, my three favourite bands were..

1. _____
2. _____
3. _____

POPPY - YOU HAVE A STORY TO SHARE

When I was young, I regret not...

_____
_____
_____
_____
_____

When I was a teenager, I earned some money by....

_____
_____
_____
_____
_____

When I left home for the first time, I went and lived....

_____
_____
_____
_____
_____

POPPY - YOU HAVE A STORY TO SHARE

These are the lessons I learnt as a teenager that I wish to pass onto my children and grandchildren.

___

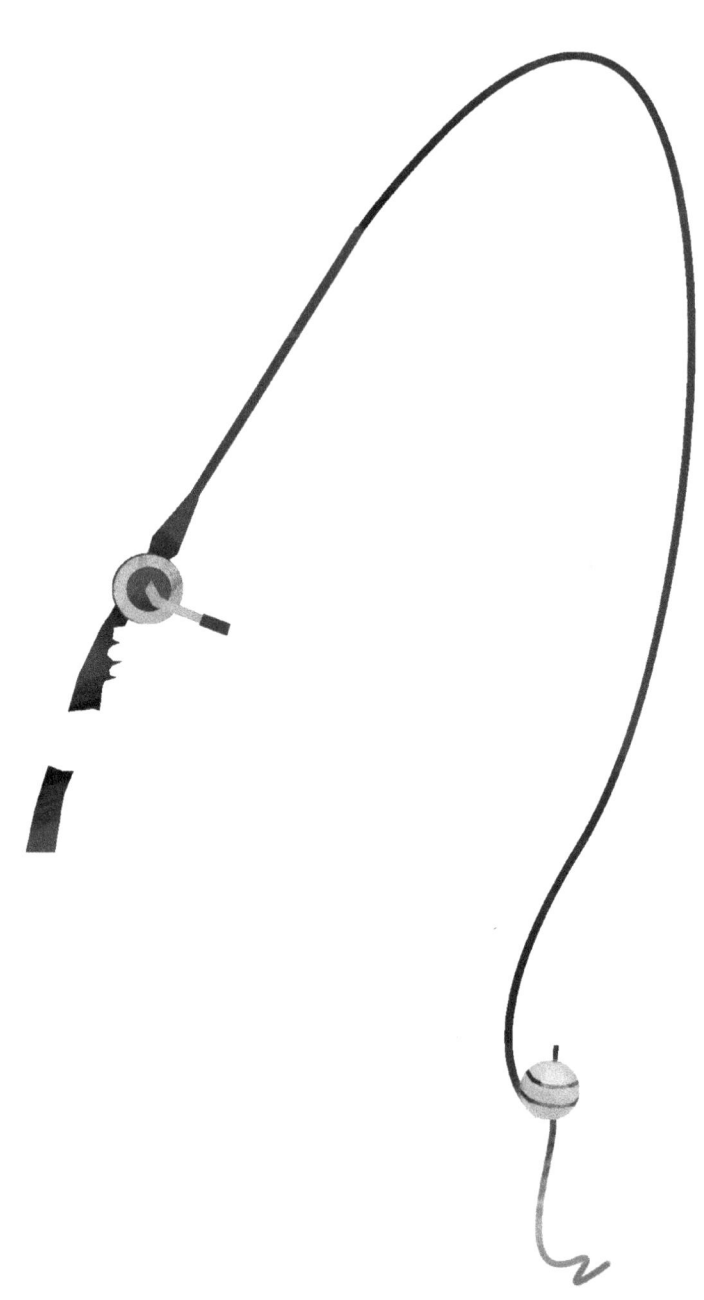

SECTION FOUR
PARENTHOOD

POPPY - YOU HAVE A STORY TO SHARE

BECOMING A PARENT

My age when I first became a parent _____

Where were you living when you became a first time parent?

Explain how you felt emotionally when you became a parent?

Was there anything that you were under-prepared for?

POPPY - YOU HAVE A STORY TO SHARE

My employment when I had my first child.

_____
_____
_____
_____

If you have other children, list the locations and dates they were born.

Name	Location	D.O.B
_____	_____	_____
_____	_____	_____
_____	_____	_____
_____	_____	_____
_____	_____	_____
_____	_____	_____
_____	_____	_____

How many children had you planned to have?

_____
_____
_____

POPPY - YOU HAVE A STORY TO SHARE

What has been your biggest challenge as a parent?

_____
_____
_____
_____
_____
_____
_____
_____
_____
_____

What are 3 key responsibilities do you believe are important as a parent?

1. _____

2. _____

3. _____

POPPY - YOU HAVE A STORY TO SHARE

BECOMING A GRANDPARENT

What year did you first become a grandparent? _____

What was the name of your first grandchild? _____

If you have more than one grandchild, list their names below.

_____ _____
_____ _____
_____ _____
_____ _____
_____ _____
_____ _____

Share a special memory of when you first became a grandparent.

_____
_____
_____
_____
_____
_____
_____
_____
_____
_____

POPPY - YOU HAVE A STORY TO SHARE

Do you have a grandparent nickname? _____

What do you enjoy most about being a grandparent?
_____
_____
_____
_____
_____

What advice would you give to your grandchild/grandchildren?
_____
_____
_____
_____
_____
_____
_____
_____

POPPY - YOU HAVE A STORY TO SHARE

Use these pages to include some parenting or grandparenting photos

POPPY - YOU HAVE A STORY TO SHARE

Use these pages to include some parenting or grandparenting photos

SECTION FIVE
LIFE, TRAVEL AND ADVENTURE

POPPY - YOU HAVE A STORY TO SHARE

If I could travel anywhere in the world for a holiday, I would visit..
_____

I would choose this location because..
_____
_____
_____
_____
_____

The activity or hobby that I enjoy most to participate now in is..
_____
_____

You could call it my '**super-power**', but I have the unique ability to be able to….
_____
_____
_____
_____
_____

POPPY - YOU HAVE A STORY TO SHARE

My biggest fear is....

If I could invite 3 famous people to dinner (deceased or alive), they would be...

1.
2.
3.

If you could re-live and experience a personal moment in your life again, it would be?

POPPY - YOU HAVE A STORY TO SHARE

Not many people would know this about me, so let me share it with you.

_____
_____
_____
_____
_____
_____
_____

If I could re-live and experience a moment in history (a world event), it would be..

_____
_____
_____
_____
_____
_____

POPPY - YOU HAVE A STORY TO SHARE

My favourite quote of all time is.

I would recommend that everyone should read...

One day in the future, I would like to be best remembered for...

POPPY - YOU HAVE A STORY TO SHARE

In no particulart order, these are some of my proudest moments.

POPPY - YOU HAVE A STORY TO SHARE

From my 20's, these are some of the jobs that I've had.
(Include the years if they can be recalled)

YEAR	EMPLOYMENT

POPPY - YOU HAVE A STORY TO SHARE

If I could have done anything as a job, it would have been..
_____
_____

The most interesting place I have ever visited has been..
_____
_____
_____
_____
_____
_____
_____
_____
_____
_____
_____
_____

E X P L O R E

POPPY - YOU HAVE A STORY TO SHARE

I feel the best way I can help others is by..

_____
_____
_____
_____

If someone was to write a book about my life, the title of the book would be..

_____
_____

I feel happiest when..

_____
_____
_____
_____
_____
_____
_____

POPPY - YOU HAVE A STORY TO SHARE

If I had to choose another country to live in, it would be...

because...

These are 3 things that I would like to do over the next 12 months.

POPPY - YOU HAVE A STORY TO SHARE

Add any additional notes or information here..

SECTION SIX
MEMORIES AND STORIES

POPPY - YOU HAVE A STORY TO SHARE

The best family holiday I've experienced has been..

___

One of the hardest life experiences I've had to deal with was...

POPPY - YOU HAVE A STORY TO SHARE

A great roadtrip I once experienced was...

I had the best meal here and I will never forget it. In fact, I would highly recommend it!

SECTION SEVEN
MY FINAL WORDS

POPPY - YOU HAVE A STORY TO SHARE

Please include any further information, stories or moments that have not been shared throughout this journal.

_____
_____
_____
_____
_____
_____
_____
_____
_____
_____
_____
_____
_____
_____
_____
_____
_____

POPPY - YOU HAVE A STORY TO SHARE

POPPY - YOU HAVE A STORY TO SHARE

POPPY - YOU HAVE A STORY TO SHARE

Please include additional photos, letters, postcards, certificates or other memorabilia in the pages provided.

POPPY - YOU HAVE A STORY TO SHARE

POPPY - YOU HAVE A STORY TO SHARE

ABOUT THE AUTHOR

Romney Nelson is a Best-Selling author and Founder of Global Self-Publishing, where he is committed to providing the highest quality books to his customers across the globe.

www.globalselfpublishing.com

Also in the Series

Available for purchase via
www.globalselfpublishing.com/storytoshare
and all major online bookstores

Everyone Has a Story to Share

www.ingramcontent.com/pod-product-compliance
Lightning Source LLC
LaVergne TN
LVHW070206080526
838202LV00063B/6567